On the Road

By Don Kilby

Kids Can Press

Trucks are the huge, heavy, hardworking machines of the road. You can feel the ground shake as they rush by, hauling loads to places near and far. Climb aboard for a close-up look at trucks on the road.

A big rig growls slowly up the ramp and onto the highway. Up front, the powerful **tractor** does the pulling. Behind, the long **trailer** carries the cargo. Because of its tremendous weight, this **tractor trailer** rolls along on thirty-four tires!

CB radio

mirror

steering wheel

bed

High up in the cab of the tractor, the driver has a clear view of the road ahead. The huge steering wheel guides the big rig. Large mirrors show what's beside the rig and behind it — especially important when backing up! Some trucks even have a cozy bed behind the seats where the driver can rest while on long trips. The CB radio keeps the driver in touch with other truckers.

There are many kinds of trailers. Each one has a special job to do. A **tanker trailer** transports liquids like water, gasoline or even syrup. Can you guess what's inside this tanker trailer?

The **box trailer** gets its name because of its shape. All sorts of goods, from bicycles and breakfast cereals to stereos and skateboards, are shipped by box trailer. Inside this box trailer, thousands of fresh-picked oranges from the sunny south are on their way north.

Really big loads such as this carnival ride are hauled on **flat bed trailers**. When the carnival is over, the ride is taken apart and fastened onto the trailer with strong chains. Then it's off to the next town, where the ride will be set up again.

refrigerator truck

A **refrigerator truck** delivers a load of tasty ice-cream bars. Even on a hot summer day, everything inside the truck stays icy cold.

flat bed trailer

The **car carrier** was built to do one special job. It carries eleven shiny new cars at one time! The vehicles on the bottom row are unloaded first. Then the cars on the top are carefully driven down ramps built into the trailer.

Trucks can
be counted on to
work hard and go for
long distances. But sometimes they
break down. Then a powerful **wrecker truck**
is called to the rescue. The wrecker hoists up
the broken tractor and tows it to a garage for repairs.
Another tractor will pick up the trailer and finish the delivery.

The driver gears down and pulls in to the **truck stop**. Here the huge gas tanks are filled, the windshield is cleaned and each tire is checked for wear and tear. Then it's time for the driver to have a break, stretch tired legs, eat a hot lunch or enjoy a piece of pie! And soon the driver is back in his rig, rolling down the highway again.

Road construction ahead! Everyone must slow down. A signalman directs traffic past the machines at work. The old road is broken up and hauled away. A **grader** smooths the surface with its wide blade. A layer of gravel is added and then the new roadbed is ready to be paved.

roller

roller

paving machine

A **paving machine** creeps along, laying the hot, sticky asphalt. **Rollers** follow close behind, flattening the new pavement. One roller rides on rows of wide rubber tires. Another rolls along on two giant drums filled with water. The last job is to paint the lines on the new pavement.

Day and night, hardworking trucks are always on the move. When one load is dropped off, a new one is picked up, and another delivery is on its way.

Next time you're on the road, look around and see how many different types of trucks you can spot!

For my parents, Joyce and Jim Kilby

Text and illustrations © 2003 Don Kilby

Kids Can Press acknowledges the financial support of the Government of Ontario, through the Ontario Media Development Corporation's Ontario Book Initiative; the Ontario Arts Council; the Canada Council for the Arts; and the Government of Canada, through the BPIDP, for our publishing activity.

Published in Canada by
Kids Can Press Ltd.
29 Birch Avenue
Toronto, ON M4V 1E2

Published in the U.S. by
Kids Can Press Ltd.
2250 Military Road
Tonawanda, NY 14150

www.kidscanpress.com

The artwork in this book was rendered in acrylic
The text is set in Univers.

Edited by Debbie Rogosin
Designed by Marie Bartholomew
Printed and bound in China

The hardcover edition of this book is smyth sewn casebound.
The paperback edition of this book is limp sewn with a drawn-on cover.

CM 03 0 9 8 7 6 5 4 3 2 1
CM PA 06 0 9 8 7 6 5 4 3 2 1

Library and Archives Canada Cataloguing in Publication

Kilby, Don
On the road / by Don Kilby.

(Wheels at work)

ISBN-13: 978-1-55337-379-7 (bound) ISBN-10: 1-55337-379-0 (bound)
ISBN-13: 978-1-55337-986-7 (pbk.) ISBN-10: 1-55337-986-1 (pbk.)

1. Trucks—Juvenile literature. I. Title. II. Series.

TL230.15.K54 2003   j629.224   C2001-902829-6

Kids Can Press is a **corus**™ Entertainment company